Lauria/Frasca Poetry Prize 1

Talk

Talk

Matthew M. Cariello

BORDIGHERA PRESS

Library of Congress Control Number: 2019936664

Cover photo:
Factory Windows, September, 1970, from the portfolio *Paterson*, 1970
gelatin silver print; 7 9/16 c 9 9/16 in. (19.2 x 24.3 cm)
San Francisco Museum of Modern Art, Purchase through a gift of
Randi and Bob Fisher
© George Tice
photo: Don Ross

Printed in the United States.

Published by
BORDIGHERA PRESS
John D. Calandra Italian American Institute
25 West 43rd Street, 17th Floor
New York, NY 10036

Lauria/Frasca Poetry Prize 1
ISBN 978-1-59954-136-5

CONTENTS

ACKNOWLEDGMENTS

ABOUT THE AUTHOR

This book is dedicated to my wife Wendy and my children, Mia and Lou Fei; to my mother and father, Michael and Norma Jean; and to my extended family stretched out across the Italian diaspora.

Part One

. . . with words
Imposing on my tongue like obols.

—SEAMUS HEANEY

THE WINDOW
(Union City, NJ 1961)

1

Then I knew one word,
birthright's rudiment

uttered in hunger's warm room.
The sense of me without sense

in total dark, alone.
The room collapsed

and by morning I saw
I lay among the trees

beyond the open frame –
before that

there was no window.
And my word was gone.

Something came creeping
through the burnished leaves –

not me, not hunger, not milk,
not sleep, not warmth.

And I named the thing
the name it gave itself,

the sound it made
just being there,

heard it first time
clear as another's word.

Deep in the branches of morning,
the memory of birds calling.

2

When she found me clinging
to the screen two stories up,

my mother would swallow her panic,
hold my shoulders tight,

and ask me to say what I saw.
If I knew no names, she pointed

and named for me. And so articulation
was folded in words she

first spoke near my face.
Hedge ivy bricks chestnut

alleyway gate trees bucket.
That was them that was the word.

Yet an invisible counterlife
chattered in my ear as she spoke.

Car yes, but car running,
clothesline's cry, dog's cough,

sparrows dancing in the ivy.
I heard in rain the downspout's talk,

traffic lights were trading colors,
birds held up the shining wires,

the hedge was a broken green wall,
cats crept down the alley singing . . .

3

Late afternoons
when the backyard cement

was half in shadow, half
in sun, and broken puddles

of water below were etched
with contradictory houses,

when there were more bricks in a wall
than were possible to count,

when the iron gate's squeal spoke,
and the sky hid between buildings,

when an airplane's drone far above
wanted to be something inside me,

when the resonance ebbed,
when the large world surged past.

SWALLOWS

I knew that swallows
over the rooftops
fell through the sky

like bullets with love
for their targets.
I could tell when they sang

their chattering song
they were praising
the air they breathed

and the rain they drank.
I thought they were always there,
but not always visible.

I believed they never
touched the earth.
I wanted each one to see

the lonely speed
of light at dawn.
I hoped their lives

were good and not too short.
I doubted they ever saw
their own shadows.

I didn't want to be
so alone in my body,
but my body was all I knew.

DELICATESSEN

The knob's click and door's creak,
newspapers stacked in rows
along the broken tiles,
pickle barrels spilling brine,
rusted fruit, and a dozen loaves

wrapped in brown paper sleeves,
heaped beyond my reach. These
were the summer evenings
on my father's heels
along the city streets –

before we moved, but I could
read, or believed I could read.
Within the frosted glass I saw
the rolls and squares of meat
and cheese, and twisted brown fish

whose eyes were out. I conceded
to their syntax, broke-in my tongue
on words caught on the palate,
scraped across teeth stretched
across breath: peppered mackerel,

cappicola, mortadella, provolone . . .
I saw the names, and saw them as if,
figured from hunger, they met
the teeth and told them what to do:
prosciutto, pastrami, kalamata, calamari.

Along the sawdust track
that crept beneath the back room's
curtain, another man emerged
as unlike my father
as I could imagine.

Black hair and beard salt
and peppered, eyes like two olives,
his nose large as a kaiser roll.
There was a clammy taint
about his apron, a marrow-essence,

a smudge of blood on his arm.
He laughed, and I shrank behind
my father's thighs. All talk
is lost in grammarless memory.
In my father's footsteps,

I watched the rituals of commerce
among the freezer cases –
wallet's flip, chime of coin,
the stiff brown bag,
top end rolled cigar-tight,

hanging from his hand.
The incense of cigarettes.
Before the street
the neon arc buzzed ИƎSSƎTAƆIˌƎD.
I wondered what it meant,
that sudden yearning toward

curves of light, an appetite
blessed by circumstance.
Then I saw I was inside. The walls,
their shelves, the rows of cans
and bottles and paper-wrapped provisions,

the quiet meats and cheeses,
the refrigerator, my father
and the other man, the antipodal
sign itself, all breathed, or seemed
to breathe, or mutter, or stumble

toward articulations I couldn't
yet imagine. We left the way we'd come,
but everything had changed – first,
I was alone, despite my father's
warm, firm hand. Each car that passed

seemed burdened with its own
immobile bulk, each house sat
harsh and bright and dumb,
every stranger's face smiled
with a kind of gentle stupidity

I shouldn't have seen for years.
And the filthy, fecund street,
unending gate-latched iron fences,
factories of proud bricks piled
high to nowhere with windows . . .

Who could sleep? And yet I slept,
and dreamed that words could crack,
break on my tongue, fix broken thought,
catch time and keep it still,
and care for sense with assonance.

THE FIG TREE IN MY GRANDFATHER'S VOICE

I know who I am.
I sit and drink wine.
My family comes

and I kiss
everyone, then
fall asleep.

It is my right!
At dinner someone
will not eat.

I am not hungry
he says –
but there is food!

They might learn
sometime, might not.
The fig tree

in the backyard –
this is the tree
of my parents and

my children also.
In August the figs
purple and split

lie here on
the kitchen table.
My family –

they say
you have lived long!
I say live as

long as you like but
don't get old.
They are so

stupid they weep.
I put a fig
in each of their

mouths and
tell them to shut up.

FOUNDATION

Clutter in the vestibule
where steps buckled
and mortar cracked.
I watched my father
crawl into the dark
beneath the stoop
to prop up a failure
in the foundation
with a moment of faith
across the gap –
steel pipe, chicken
wire and cement.
I peered within the space
between holding-up and
breakthrough, learned
the way he'd brace
himself to the tasks
at hand. A muttered
phrase or sigh or
whistle, the tapping
foot, crossed arms,
the sharp echo
and flash and smoke
of a match struck
before his face to meet
the cigarette's judgment.
At times his patience
cracked, for this job
wasn't his work.
The reluctant hammer slipped,
the trowel gouged when
it should have smoothed,
underpinnings he'd
constructed slipped

and tore. I watched
and learned to watch,
and wait, and rebuild
what had been razed
and razed again.
After three days among
the dust and chiseling,
coughs and scuffs and scrapes
of wet cement,
he emerged white as ash,
beating dust from
his body, laughing,
shielding his eyes
against the light.

TALK

At times my mother's tongue
would fix itself.
Away from family,
she'd lose the glottal stop

she'd gotten from the street,
dropped Rs began to rise,
syllables drawn
in sharp spoken clicks.

As if diction marked
sophistication,
she'd make the impression,
and by that fiction shield herself

from other people's opinion.
It just happened. It wasn't subtle.
Among half-strangers
or those for whom the language

of protocol is essential,
she'd speak correctly, clearly,
carefully. Sometimes,
she'd surprise herself

with what she said
under such pretensions.
"I think I have to disagree."
"The sky is certainly

inspirational tonight,
isn't it?" "What a lovely table."
This might seem funny.
But when her speech was clipped,

cut-up by antagonists,
those close-cropped consonants
broke new ground. Listeners stopped,
cocked their heads, attention caught.

BIRCH

I was just out of the city,
not yet in school, the kind of boy
whose knees were always muddy,
who disappeared for hours just
at dusk, who brought home
small things: acorns, stones,
seedpods, feathers, the odd
amphibian. The patch of woods
near the school was my home,
and the meadow beside it too,
filled with high grass that toppled
in autumn like yellow hair
that had been parted by wind.
Once, beside the black-bottomed
drainage ditch that circled
the field, I found a birch.
It was late in the year.
First frost had mown the grass.
No leaf clung to the branch-tips,
or a few that gripped with
desperate yellow devotion.
It was nothing I had ever seen before,
an inadvertent fullness, a moment
of certainty—I wanted to be
that slip of birch at the ditch's
edge. I knew I could live there near
the lip of flat water that took
leaves back down. I climbed the tree
and as I climbed it bent and kept
bending down the water's scaffold.
Broken with ripples, my own face
shone in blackish water.
It seemed like rising,
but everything to root must go.
How long I spent on that bent

trunk, I don't know. But even
now in every birch I see
my initials hacked, the gnarled
stretch of bark that droops
along the cusp of a C,
the heavy bend that caught
my weight and held it
above the deep black ditch
sown with dead leaves.

THE RIDE

Again, the hilltop's top.
I knew my eyes
would tear, the trip
back up took hours,
but flattened my body
to the run, threw
my weight into it,
fell past lights and
faces, felt the dull
thud on bumps when
snow rose in plumes
from runners.
I fell through night
like I'd never stop,
slide on and on,
no street to scrape,
no rope to pull,
no height to climb.
When speed had cut
the wind I pushed
my hands, had wings
in snow, my eyes
saw stars stars stars.
Over I rolled, broke
my long fall softly
in a soft drift.
Easy in the snow,
I wanted to sleep.
My two hands fluttered
in the air above.
My frozen breath rose
like music, stiffened,
swayed above my body.
I knew it. It
was easy. It was
this easy to die.

OLD YORK BOOKS
(New Brunswick, NJ 1977)

Stealing study time from school,
I'd pace the ransacked shelves,
tip trembling waist-high piles,
skim slanted tables filled

with broken used-up musty books.
Among the chaos of mediocrities,
I'd make a stack of future reading,
then sit and brush away the dust.

Enveloped in the must, I couldn't read.
Each book turned in my hands, opened,
then words would dim, sentences
bleed, the names and places fade.

Beyond the store's one window, autumn
was coming on, or had already come.
The day was bright, or it was raining.
Something would happen. I was waiting

for the books to speak, the lines
to unstring themselves all at once,
the stacks to tumble – clarity, evidence,
anything at all as confirmation

of my selections. The books were mute
as the owner's wife, whose disheveled
wall-eyed stare fixed both me and the door.
Eventually I'd leave the store wrecked

with indecision. It would soon be spring,
or winter. I would be alone or in love.
The books would keep. I returned often.
I swore I'd never go back again.

FIRST JOB

That first summer from college,
aged twenty-three,
I worked a hard job.

After sweaty sleep,
sheets clinging to skin,
her arm loose on my side,

I'd rise for work
(she'd never see me leave),
and stop for plums, purple,

stems attached, a leaf or two.
The first I'd eat walking,
bitter snapping skin sticking

on my palate. At the warehouse,
I'd peel covers from books,
half tear them through,

place torn books in boxes,
leave them on the platform.
Twenty boxes a day,

the odd sweep-up.
The platform stunk of rot,
spoiled milk, crumbling paper.

Broken books moldered.
A plum peeled my mouth clean,
the yellow pulp and pit red as sex

stuck in my throat,
made me blink and turn away.
The rest of them I'd save –

a bag on the kitchen table,
two or three hard fruit
left to scold her mouth.

A HANGOVER FOR MY FATHER

You begin the day same
as last – walk dog,
fix coffee, watch for paper.

Sun begins to hang from trees,
angling up the clapboard,
crossing panes, creasing glass.

I'm still knocked out.
Last night we cracked
the scotch, drank too much,

got pissed too soon,
talked loud and hard.
I asked a lot.

You fill a second cup.
The kitchen table creaks.
You talked about the army,

Germany in '53, rain
and waking in dark barracks,
cognac, cards and platinum blondes.

Black coffee shimmers,
the echo trembles
through your finger

hooked in the handle.
You wonder what you said,
what secrets cracked the patch

of ground between us.
The horizon is clear now,
cut with light, sun high as a house.

When I stagger, yawning,
to the kitchen,
the silence pains us both.

THE BOY AND THE TREE

He pulls down leaves, pulls leaves from trees
and dreams of sheaves of light, burning leaves,

each red and gold and white as ash, or fire,
and countless as stars in sleep. The leaves,

I say, are yours to keep. But while he gleans,
the fall comes on. His leaves are lost with other leaves

from other trees that crossed his own.
It isn't fair. So many many leaves

have fallen, can't be caught or touched or found.
Leave them rot there, let them molder,

or I'll go blind with shadow-raking
light no eyes can see. The boy is sorry: for all his trying,

for all the sheaves he pulls from trees,
for all his dreams of leaves beneath

the ground, burning, for all his leaving
things unsaid, losing things, his sleeping.

Part Two

Se que
no
van a creerme
pero
canta,
canta la sal, la piel
de las salares,
canta . . .

—PABLO NERUDA

A LONG STORY

The shore forces the sea,
      the broken sun sinks,
            clouds crowd the horizon.

To remember, we forget
      we invent small stories.
            In a new land, sun

and moon compromise
      through shifting dunes –
            a long story,

and I pretend to know
      just one chapter at a time.
            When trapped in the grammar

of the moment, improvise:
      the willet's footprint
            etched in sand,

the machinery of the passing wind,
      a cipher set before
            the tongue.

If I speak in the bell's mouth,
      break remaining sound,
            what's left to hold?

Incipient
      silence inchoate
            voice.

THE BIRDS AT NESEQUAGH

in the empty school
parking lot
five different birds call

Cardinal

The winter bird –
muted brown female,
dodgy red male –
but the clear piping
of summer remains.
They inspect the low scrub
and bushes – the stuff of berries
and hard seeds they crack at will,
split open and eat
and can't shut up about it.

Pigeons

Pigeons are tough,
relentless in their apparent
stupidity.
They coo and croon
outside the library window
and won't be let in.
They're proud of their ancestors
and the great tradition
of ignorance.
Incestuous, they never know
the real value of money.

Mockingbird

The mockingbird dances
at the top

of a telephone pole.
He flashes and wheels
his flashy feathers
and dives at the cat.

I don't believe I will die
I don't believe I will die
I don't believe the world is round
I am a hundred colors
of grey and white
I can hear the sun rise
You can learn from me
but I won't teach you a thing
I don't believe I will die
I don't believe I will die

Ring-Neck Pheasant

In the wood it sings
so few so few
silently to itself.
It carries the painful look
of one too beautiful
but not smart enough.
Awkward and resolute,
it will sit motionless
for hours, while the day
dies of boredom.

Sparrows

They toss the dirt over their heads,
roll in the dust and rise
in a puff of smoke
to the ledge of the building,
then return to the dirt.

They scare easily.
They know the strength of numbers
and copulate furiously.
They love all each other equally
and wingtip to wingtip
would circle the earth.

CRICKET IN NOVEMBER

Voice of havoc,
shroud of summer
cricketing now

behind November's
stove –
what is your

feeble effort
to the declining
year?

Black box of time
singing your
machinery of light,

why bother?
You are silent
for days,

and then the heat
of the oven, the quick
replay of the sun's height

sends you chirruping
without thinking –
why?

I have taken
the descent of
winter

and made with it
a lattice of thought,
while you simply waited

and wait now simply
for the temperature
to rise,

the roast to cook,
the bread to bake,
the water to boil,

the human aroma
to rise in the kitchen.
And then you sing

tentatively,
modestly,
unbelievably,

and send me
rolling toward
my solstice sleep

unnourished
yet glowing
with the heat

of a clicking fire.
Black cricket
blasting

my green vanity,
I am all the same
to you,

trudging my way
around your
delicate liminal life.

You are my conscience
whispering constantly
nothing in particular

in the slack of the evening,
as I wait by the stove
for the heat.

THE BAT

One hair flung from a fiddle bow,
        an echo suspended in branches,
                the levitating moth

and spiraling mosquito
        are all part of him.
                His self-sense is all sensation,

a journey among simplicities,
        point to point to point.
                In the pivot of leather wings

over meadowgrass,
        he is suddenly brilliant,
                temporarily complete.

Nowhere to rest,
        built just for flight and sleep,
                he meets himself over and over

in air over earth,
        always new, always.
                How does he see himself so clearly

without recognizing sight?
        While the small bat sings,
                my nocturnal humming

in the mirror catches nothing,
        the black sky whistles back,
                soft mosquitoes buzz.

MONTAUK POINT

If you are squeamish
don't prod the beach rubble
SAPPHO

Broken on Montauk's
rocky coast
lie shells –
razor clam, whelk,
slipper shell, and
those delicate sand-spun
sailor's toenails.

Among the wrack
of sea stars and eelgrass
tossed from the water
lies a skate,
all struggle ended,
wedged in the rounded
clacking boulders
around which the sea drains.
His body is the wedge of a diamond
still wet from the sea.
A single row of thorns
runs along
the middle of his back;
the sloping slender tail
descends to a point.

I squat above him.
My instinct is
to flip him over,
examine his underside
pink and stippled,
his angled snout
and downturned mouth,

red and petalled.
His eyes –
I suppose
they are his eyes –
are shut.

Everything else
on that coast
is shattered.
The ocean has cut the cliff
behind us,
breaking dune and earth,
taking beachgrass,
pine and plum and rose
to a place I can't see.

The skate lay still.
If my fingers
could find the breadth
of his solid flesh,
touch the shape
of his wide wing,
I would feel the sea
rush around me
and the roar
in my ears
would quiet
to a murmur.

A DANCE OF TUGBOATS
(for Charles Norman Bausch, captain of the Elmira)

they fog the harbor with sighs,

glossy grey,
shuddering like bells
under their own weight,
                    converge
red-stacked, tire wrapped,
heavy in their love
                    for water –
up to their necks
in it –
                    floating steel
aching for the sea.

they scatter
like workers in a field,
                    each bending
with a full load,
                    half sunken
in the earth
                    they carry
a harvest of stones
                    across the river
and return
                    with a harvest of sand.
at the edge
                    of open water,
the edge of the sea,
the harbor's wordless mouth,
they wait,
iron bound by the bounds
of land,
                    cracked

and shivering,
and return with the tide,
                              almost lovely,
almost silent
almost –

like swans, ready to fly

JELLYFISH

You are the cup of the sea,
water woven
into filaments of light,
a star etched
on broken water's edge.
I lay beside you
listening
to the ocean arrive.
A crescent moon
leaves the water
like a sail
and lifts itself
to the sky.
The wave
that carried you
to the sand
has crawled back
to its foamy bed and
deadly tendrils extended,
you die.

I can't throw you back.
You die
without thought
with some small spark of life
and will dry to dust
in a day.
I won't miss you
and soon you'll be gone
gone –
my venomous balloon,
holy water,
radiant stone,
lidless eye, moon, blood.

A BULB OF GARLIC

Citadel, catacomb,
sculpted shadow's stone.
In each clove's cleft
are miles of open air.
The redolence of lilies
fills its crevices.
Along the arc of its flank,
red-flecked veins spin
among fleshened curves,
purling toward the shank
that sends the leaf toward light.
Patient and self-satisfied
(a rudiment of appetite),
it talks in the mouth:
Clove by clove you take me,
down to my green pith.
I settle in your heart's blood.
When you die I am content
having spent my life
in soil no stone ever knew.

GLASS OF BEER

Its foamy borders
circle perfectly.

A glistening,
a liquid reckoning
of greatness
bubbles up
from some well –
a breath
of the heart.

A yellow sea.
On the surface
floats an island.
In the middle is a volcano.
The island is uncharted
and wanders among the continents.

See the tiny people
who live there –
they are your cousins
favorite uncle
unmarried sister
and your mother and father
as children.

They live on the grain
as gods live
timeless
in the revolving sea.
Their whole world
is a yellow ocean
held

in a clear glass –
the glass you enter
to live their lives.

ODE TO MY TIE

The flower of my youth,
the road to the west,
the knotted root of oak,

you, my tie, caress
the last waves at sunset.
You go round

and round.
You ask for forgiveness
but expect nothing.

Once you lived
in shadowed halls
of coliseums

but now the first thing
every day is the kind
windowed light of spring.

You reach for me.
I hold you like a child.
Every night

we sleep apart,
old lovers remembering
another spring, another life.

STONE MAN
Meditations on an Inuit Figure

Stone Man Watches Fire

The world is mostly water,
but drop me in the flame
and I wont burn,
I wont even sing.
Fire burns only
what can't keep,
and burning, sends it away.
At the heart of it
I'll stand barrel-chested,
my shoulders square
with the hearth.
I'll grow red as blood.
In morning you'll dig me
from the ashes, touch
my smooth perfect skin,
and my burning light
will caress and wound you.

Stone Man Sleeps

I dreamed hands
tended to my body,
rubbed me clean
with oil from their skin,
shined me with
the fur of a seal,
and set me facing east.
When the sun rose,
my shadow grew long
and strode across the snow.
There I found a man
whose body of flesh and blood
had melted into light.

Seeing the shadow
I threw, his eyes
rolled back in his head,
but his hands,
grasping my shoulders,
shone like stars.

Stone Man Wants a Mate

Wear me in your belly
and I will keep you warm.
Nurtured, I nurture.
Borne, I bear.
I watch your sleep
and fire your dreams.
My unbroken form
is a solid longing
for your love.
I am the echo
of your mortality.
While you live,
I will flourish.
When you die,
I will grow silent,
introspective, and
keep your house
forever.
I am
your twin,
your lover,
elemental.
I spell your fears.
I live your life.

Stone Man Watches Snow

Once I too was buried
in the sameness of my fellows,

but now I am singular.
I was plucked from the earth.
I was carved by the mind of a man,
then by his hand tossed
across the sea.
My weight keeps me
here on the ground,
completely surrounded
by only myself.
I have been subsumed
into time, at the heart
of the weather, yet removed.
The snow goes where it will,
the trees bend in the wind,
break and die.
But I am not rooted,
not part of the earth anymore.
Snow, dirt, rock.
Flesh, earth, stone.
My place is set
among the fractured
crystals of drifting stars.

Stone Man Sees the Moon

My mirror, my mother,
sky-opal – is this
the womb from which
I dropped? Is this
my father's face?
My head is eternally
uplifted -- am I
listening to you?
Are you looking for your children,
pulling the envelope of the sea
constantly from its rocks,
searching the black crevices,

leaving on the waters your likeness?
You come big over the sea
and mountains every day,
then diminish and sink
pitifully. I am here!
See me and I will
leap into your light –
stone for stone,
planet for planet.
Your light burns
my face and whispers
over cold boulders of the earth.
So much mist –
so much to block my way.

Stone Man Listens

Mute, polished ice,
burnished stone.
I alone am both silent
and still.
In me flow colors
of the sea, transfixed,
permanent, level
with the ocean surface.
In me swells
the hurricane wave,
hard and unloving.
But it will not fall.
I am a sure weight –
I am stone
but will not sink
or float or settle
on the earth's bed.

Again, I am lifted
in the man's hand,

brought to the light
before his face.
He is whispering.
What are these words?
What is my life to him?
Beyond all this,
my crystalline breath
contracts, sharpens,
and in me explode suns.

THE PEN

putting   ink to paper
  his   hand became the
  pen   turning letters
seeing   beneath the page
  to   words that formed there
  his   hand became the
  pen   poised above the page
 half   touching paper
 half   beneath the page
turning   letters
 until   he formed letters
 when   hand became the pen
words   that waited there
 were   ink above the page
  in   the pen within the hand and
words   said what letters
meant   but beneath the page
beyond   the hand poised there
ready   to become pen
within   the hand within the pen

Part Three

Oh I cannot say it. There is no word.

—WILLIAM CARLOS WILLIAMS

SONG

By this bird again, my child listening,
this two-note call from memory

among March's snowpatch memory,
childlike, insisting the bird is calling back.

Born in snow, born in Spring, born
in March's snowpatch, memory's

soluble insistence, grey as sifting
ash blowing in the shifting wind.

The child listening, the bird declaring
morning among the shaft of sun.

This two-note call becoming
the memory of that song in snow,

in Spring, melting. My child almost
answering his sister's voice already

before she calls the bird a bird.
Silence intervenes. The call of morning's

years across two notes. Two notes:
the memory of birds and birds.

And hands like birds in sunlight,
falling. This two-note call from memory

among March's snowpatch memory.

MEMENTO MORI

Beside the sign above the door
is a two-man cross-cut saw,
ancient teeth bent
and broken, rusted
nearly clean through in spots.

And this is what's left,
the difference of being
from having – a player piano
stripped of its ivory,
the lid unhinged,

but it "still runs."
Or a mantle, disassembled
from the wall, the entire home
that held it fallen to rubble.
There are mirrors

that don't mirror,
drawers that won't open,
doors that won't swing,
lamps and lanterns
that won't light.

What to do with it? Innumerable
rusted useless tools, time-frozen
clamps and springs, a funnel,
a pump, an electric motor,
a breathless leather bellows.

And here are the dolls.
Here are their limbs, torsos,
clothes, shoes and cradles.
Here is bowl of doll eyes.
Here's a clock without a key.

And a pile of family photos,
austere faces suffering
the long stillness before
the camera's flash, still
waiting to be told it's safe

to move. Amid the rubble and dross
and waste of a hundred years,
crudely carved from waste-wood,
capped with a cruder cover,
a foot-long casket,

inscribed "memento mori."
Inside, carefully folded
over and plaited with love
and tied with ribbons
now frayed and brown,

two feet of scarlet hair,
not a vein of grey among it –
the difference of having
from being. Whose hands
touched her hair at that

last moment before leaving
forever? Who thought
of sharpening the knife
so as not to tear,
but sever cleanly and keep

the memory of death,
which means remembering life?
And where are those hands now?
Which shelf? Which box?
Behind what unspeakable door

were they driven hard down
by the ruinous world
toward that permanent
clattering collected silence,
shattered and fast and perfect.

MASTER BUKKO, THE NUN MUJAKU,
AND THE BUCKET WITHOUT A BOTTOM

Mujaku asked master Bukko
"What is the teacher
doing who writes words?"

He said, "To a deaf man,
you show the moon by pointing.
To a blind man,

you show the moon
by tapping on the wall."
When she found the moon

in her water bucket,
Mujaku made a poem,
and took it to the master.

"Where is that light?"
said Bukko. She looked up.
A deer coughed at the edge

of the wood.
When Bukko said
"Who is that listening?"

Mujaku stood.
For this one articulation,
Mujaku was allowed

to meet the master all winter,
until the bucket bottom broke.
With feet still wet she said

"The bottom fell out

of my bucket. Now it holds
no water, nor the moon.

What really is the bucket
without a bottom?"
Bukko was silent.

Among Mujaku's words,
the moon descended,
and kept descending,

and knocked itself to splinters.

THE LAST WAVE

Then I sat at the kitchen table while outside
a thousand foot wave approached.

It was on the news; everyone knew it
was coming. My parents had long since

stopped running, whereas I had just
arrived carrying my daughter, for whom

every new thing was still an adventure.
The sky darkened, the vast rumbling

grew louder. I wondered at their complacency,
and although my first concern

was for my child, I knew I wanted
to keep living also. And yet again

I knew that there was no tomorrow
to make up for what had been already lost.

Then the ground began to shake.
The last thing I remember is the smoke

from my parents' cigarettes rising
calmly in the air of the doomed kitchen,

and my daughter amazed at it all.

ORIENTATION

"Before I go to bed
I have to orient myself —
Which way is north?
Where do my feet point?

Where will the sun rise?
Once, on the Cape
I couldn't remember,
or couldn't figure

which way was which.
We had come from south,
but turned and turned.
Your sister was an infant,

remember? You had stitches
on your knee and walked
too close to the cliffs.
I tossed all night,

listened to your father's groans
next to me, your breathing,
got up to check your sleep,
and Amy, I touched her hair —

it was still so fine, she was newborn,
I remember that so well . . .
(Remember
the day she came home?

I said 'You can pet her,
but remember, never touch
that soft spot in the middle
of her head, right *there*'.)

I sat at the window until dawn,
smoking, wondering
where it would happen,
and when. And as I sat

I imagined myself sitting,
watching myself wondering. Odd.
Years later, I had that feeling
again, when we had to go

collect her body.
It was like a stage,
the lights arranged just so —
and actors just standing,

posed, not talking,
but all in green,
with masks half off,
and just standing,

not talking but watching
us come into the room.
There was nothing else there.
She was on a table in the middle.

It was like someone else's life,
like I saw myself from above.
They weren't my hands that traced
the curves of her quiet body,

just a little sign of life left
around the bend of her lips,
and the way she was still warm
on my palms.

And her feet —
she has her father's feet
I always said,
so who's feet does her father have?

Funny I should think that then.
When we left the place,
everything outside was still the same,
the smokestacks blowing on the Turnpike,

the trucks cutting us off.
Your father so calm, remembering
to turn here, watch out for this fork,
get in the right lane."

WHILE RAKING LEAVES IN THE AUTUMN OF MY 45TH YEAR, I THINK OF LI BAI GETTING DRUNK IN THE MORNING

Between long rows of fences
trees shed their light.

The cat goes missing all night,
then shows up with a dove in its mouth.

The sun shines for an hour,
then rain chases me indoors.

After three days, my wife
and child return from a journey.

Someday I'll lie beneath the sky
and let leaves be my blanket.

HUNTER'S MOON

Remembering, I sigh; looking ahead, I sigh once more.
LI BAI

The river reaches the edge
of the dam, pauses, then falls.

The Hunter's Moon hesitates,
low and red in the western sky.

Ignatow said that love
is the beginning of fear.

What is the beginning of love?
Also fear, but a different kind.

~ ~

Li Bai sat by a small stream
and remembered the Yangtze.

He stood on the Yangtze's banks
and longed for his own small stream.

I've always feared depth greater
than my height: what indulgence!

~ ~

I buy two books and leave them
next to my bed for three years, unread.

I sleep with an open window
to hear thieves in the street.

One night, someone breaks in,
takes my books and reads them.

~ ~

Among the bricks stacked beside the garage,
once again, sadly, autumn crickets.

After napping happily all day,
I fitfully walk my rooms all night.

The streetlights make little orange pools
on the streets where no one walks.

The words of crickets in autumn –
how many years have they been talking?

~ ~

Spread beneath a chestnut tree,
this year's fallen harvest, ignored.

I'm halfway through this life,
wasting my time trying to be smart.

~ ~

And that sycamore outside my window –
it must be depressed, too.

I stay awake deep into the night,
listening to the leaves not moving.

Trying to catch the essence
of things, I miss their resonance.

~ ~

Each morning all summer,
the same blue heron stood at the pond's edge.

And each morning I saw the bird

as I ran by, and saluted her.

One morning it was gone, but by then
I'd already stopped seeing it.

~ ~

Thousands of starlings rattle
the maple outside my window.

I avoid a few large difficulties
to settle for many small ones.

I could clap my hands and make them fly,
but in a few moments they'd be back.

I lean back as the dusk comes on,
listen to the clamor of falling leaves.

~ ~

The cat climbs the fence
with a dove in his mouth,

and when he drops it to show me,
the bird flies up to the roof.

I watch the dove until it's gone,
but the cat hoards his mouthful of feathers.

If this life is a dream, why
do I drink so much wine?

~ ~

In the tall grass beside the river,
an abandoned car rusts contentedly.

It's that time again – one by one
leaves gather in the gutters.

Last night there were shouts on the street,
cars racing, the sad smell of gasoline.

Today it rains, and the rain comes down,
and all roads lead to the river.

~ ~

After midnight, the rain clears out;
tonight will have a killer frost.

As if the moon is always out ahead of me,
always behind, moving when I move.

We sit in the chilly silence
until only the moon remains.

THE SHOVEL

It lived in this house before me,
moldering in the cellar's damp,
its handle ground to fit the clench
of other fingers, the blade bent right

from someone else's harsh use.
Old earth dredged by another's labor
is wedged in the dented metal.
Before my time, this tool felt

the heel's kick, rasp of soil,
carved dirt with its straight
and bent edges, tapers and flares,
the ache of its hardwood shaft.

I heft it in my hands. No balance here,
no aim, no spin in throbbing silence,
just shove and scrape and reluctant gouge.
This tool has no appetite for earth.

Its time past, the riveted steel creaks,
the brace shudders at my grip.
Nothing left for it now
but excavation of the other side.

BIRTHDAY POEM

Halfway through this life,
wondering about the path
that begins in tall grass,
and meanders, the story goes,
past the dunes and roses to the vast ocean,
undulating and serene.

I've been there before, time and again
expecting to see something new
along the horizon: a simple mistake.
A distant point where lines of nothing converge.
Behind me, the scent of roses.
Before me, the smell of the sea.

THE STUMP

Before frost set that Fall,
he sweated wood, broke its grain,
split its strength against the coming cold.
Solid blocks of rock maple
carved from the once-tall trunk
became armloads of heat and steam,
shadow of smoke across the roof.
That should have been enough.
But hard into winter, the importance
of cords stacked along the southern wall
diminished in his mind.
Instead of keeping to his fire,
or staying in the kitchen tending dinner,
he stood before the window
and weighed what remained
until his breath caught on the glass
and hardened to sharp crystals.
He should have left the stump alone.
Alone with springing green sweetness
that struck back, numbing hands,
his arms would ache from extending the axe
to its full slicing length,
each swing risking an eye, a foot,
airborne splinters circling
the stump, sticking in grass.
Hours spent ringing the blade
against bowed heartwood
left his hands bent, as if clutching
the round of a handle in sleep.
And still the knotted root stood,
concentrically opposed to his task,
taking the axe as a palm takes money,
holding it to keep against weather.
When first snow softened the land's

jagged edges, he began to understand
what can't be broken must be coaxed.
Around the stump he piled brush and boughs,
waited until dusk and set the fire.
In open palms he felt the flame
fly down the path of roots, breath of ash
that left the ground so easily,
as did his daughter in flowers and incense.
His sleep is not as easy, split
by the ache and creak of limbs
swaying overhead swinging over
and over down and down.

MY MOTHER AT THE EDGE OF TREES

At woods' edge,
she watches for her father
who lost his voice, his sense,
his memory of the children

hauled on his shoulders.
She waits for his heavy step.
She sees her mother,
bent with birthing, who kept

her life-scraps safely hidden
to take them out at the last.
She shakes her head, touches bark.
"It's what you can't see or name,

what escapes that's most scary,
or what you see, but too late
to change or recognize."
She calls all names the same

then says that nothing
is really nameable—not
where she lives, who she sees,
how she feels or what she says.

My mother watches the slow roll
of the earth toward dark.
She's out in the field,
gathering wood for the season

called silence.
She points to the ground,
or sky, then remembers something,
turns and waves.

The arms of her red coat
spin in the breaking dusk.

ON THE BATTENKILL

This morning, morning's river
rippled beneath our paddles.

Willows doubled their height
in the rippling water

and we paddled slowly
downstream together,

my parents and my children.
We passed banks bright

with goldenrod, clover,
wild carrot, and cicadas.

Pulled by the deep current,
our boats kept moving,

while above, thunderheads
passed silently along

and herons headed home.
Don't disappear, I thought.

Let's be like the fish
who never leave the stream.

Let's be like the dragonflies
that touch the river's surface

and move on but not too far.
My mother and daughter both

wondered where we were.
We're here, I wanted to say,

but didn't. When it was time to dock,
I struggled the boat to shore

just before the current
grew too strong.

ON NOT EATING THE LAST FIG OF THE YEAR

Cut as a sprig
from my grandfather's garden,

for forty years
the tree has followed me

around the country,
each pot bigger than the last.

Two hundred figs this summer,
all incense in my mouth.

Now it's nearly October.
Beneath a leaf, one last ripeness.

Each fig is every fig.
I take it without moving.

ACKNOWLEDGMENTS

The poems in this collection have appeared in *Poet Lore, Ailanthus, Artful Dodge, The Evening Street Review, The Moth, Voices in Italian Americana, Ovunque Siamo, Café Review, Poets against the War,* & others.

ABOUT THE AUTHOR

MATTHEW M. CARIELLO was born and raised in New Jersey. One morning in 1962 as he stood in the cement backyard in Union City, an airplane flew overhead and the drone of the plane's engine harmonized with some frequency deep in his brain. He attended Rutgers as an undergrad and the Master's program in creative writing at New York University, and earned a PhD in English Education from NYU in 1992. He was fortunate enough to work with dozens of remarkable poets and teachers during his years in New York and New Jersey, and made maybe five good friends. His first book of poems, *A Boat That Can Carry Two/ Una barca per due*, won the 2010 Bordighera Poetry Prize and was published in a bilingual edition in 2011. He's had stories, haiku, poems and reviews published in *Voices in Italian Americana, Ovunque Siamo, Poet Lore, The Moth, Artful Dodge, The Evening Street Review, Modern Haiku, Frogpond, Heron's Nest, The Long Story, Atlas Poetica, Under the Basho, The Indiana Review, Iron Horse Review, The Journal*, and others. Currently, he's a senior lecturer in the English department at The Ohio State University in Columbus, where he teaches courses in literature and writing.

LAURIA/FRASCA POETRY PRIZE
The prize was conceived to promote the poetry of the Italian diaspora in English. Quality poetry in any style and on any theme is sought.

MATTHEW CARIELLO. *Talk*. Vol. 1. 2018 winner

www.ingramcontent.com/pod-product-compliance
Lightning Source LLC
Chambersburg PA
CBHW032049040426
42449CB00007B/1042